NO LONGER AM I A BABY MAMA...
Getting rid of that *STANK* "Baby Mama" Mentality

NO LONGER AM I A BABY MAMA

Copyright © 2017 by DeLisa New Williams
All rights reserved.

Published by:
NyreePress Literary Group
Fort Worth, TX 76161
1-800-972-3864
www.nyreepress.com

Cover and Back Photo: Billy Montgomery PhotographY
Makeup: Sheena Marie Glam Studios
Stylist: Latonya Mitts - Catrice Couture Exquisites
Models: Chausii Roberson, Kadasche Green, Taylor Jones

Interior Design:
Devyn Maher
www.doodles.blue

All rights reserved. No part of this book may be used or reproduced by any means, graphic, electronic, or mechanical, including photocopying, recording, taping or by any information storage retrieval system without the written per- mission of the publisher. Copying this book is both illegal and unethical.

ISBN print: 978-1-945304-71-2

Library of Congress Control Number: pending
Categories: Non-Fiction / Christian Living / Self-Help
Printed in the United States of America

This is NOT a book for the woman who is trying to get back with her child's father. You won't read any tips on how to get him back; he's gone, he's free, and now it's your turn to be FREE as well.

DEDICATION

This book is for every woman who wants to be set free from issues relating to their child's father. This is also for the father who wants to set the mother of their child free through understanding. I would like to thank God, and life's many experiences that have allowed me to personally be a "baby momma", and deal with "baby mommas" in many aspects of my inner and outer circles. You all have been a model for the good and bad, and have inspired me to help other people be free.

To my Husband: Thank you for allowing me into your life to learn and grow. I appreciate all the lessons learned with those who came as a packaged deal. Let's be free together in Jesus Name!!

CONTENTS

DEDICATION	i
FOREWORD	v
PREFACE	ix
A SPECIAL NOTE TO MY READERS	xii
INTRODUCTION I'm the pregnant one, not YOU!	1
CHAPTER 1 Admittance: I don't have the problem: He does!	6
CHAPTER 2 Discovery: God, SHOW me where this is coming from?	11
CHAPTER 3 Cleansing: Cleanse me from the inside out	17
CHAPTER 4 Believe/Receive: If you want to RECEIVE you have to BELIEVE	22
CHAPTER 5 You have to be STRONG	30
MOMENTS OF REALNESS	34
31 DAYS OF POSITIVE AFFIRMATIONS	35
REFERENCES	37
MEET DELISA NEW WILLIAMS	39

FOREWORD

No longer Am I A Baby's Mama, this book candidly addresses a blended/step family. A blended family is more common than ever before. The book in its own prophetic way defines what is a blended family; difficulties of blended families; and how to successfully overcome these difficulties, and how to become a strong supportive family unit. Most importantly, the text suggests blended families have benefits of two, or more caring parents to provide role models, all family members learn to appreciate diversity and differences, and emotional support can be available for all family members.

Common issues in blended families is children have a difficult time sharing parents. The text/workbook offers practical ways to resolve common issues and encourages one to understand it takes time and patience, and it gives the reader 31 days of positive affirmations.

Jesus himself was born in a blended family. Joseph was not really Jesus' father but really his step-father, so to speak, so Jesus knew what it was like having to grow up with half-brothers and sisters, having at least four brothers that we know of, James, Joseph, Simon, and Judas (Matt 13:55) and also sisters, although since they are not named, we don't know how many He had. The fact that He has "sisters" must mean that He had at least two of them (Matt 13:55).

DELISA NEW WILLIAMS

As Christians blended families are becoming more and more common. God places a very high value on family and taking care of and supporting each other. Men should manage their families well and raise children who respect them (1 Timothy 3:4). A woman should teach others what is good, carry herself modestly and submissively, and train younger women how to love their husbands and children (Titus 2:3-5). Caring for our relatives, especially those who live in our household, is of utmost importance (1 Timothy 5:8). Children should be obedient to and honor their parents, as long as the parents do not ask the children to do anything against God's will (Ephesians 6:1-3). When the children are grown, they have the responsibility to repay their parents by caring for them in their old age (1 Timothy 5:4. These principles apply equally to families, blended or not.

In closing, When two families come together to form one blended family, they are coming from different households with different rules, different traditions, and different ways of doing things. It is crucial that children are helped through the massive changes they will experience during the transition to a new, blended family life. Cooperation, patience, and communication will be key. Children must feel accepted and secure in the love of both parent and step-parent. Rules for discipline should be set up and enforced fairly for all the children.

DeLisa teaches us we should rid ourselves of the stank baby momma's mentality and always be supportive of each other; Jesus relied on His "stepfather" Joseph for companionship and support. Jesus recognized the need for a support system (Matthew 26:38) and also the need for private time to become spiritually refreshed. In a family, we should always be encouraging and uplifting. We should also be a good example of godliness and conduct ourselves with integrity and with instruction from the Lord.

Dr. Beverly Carnes-Lowe
Professor and Clinical Psychologist

Preface

On May 25, 2005, I became the mother of a beautiful daughter, and there in the room were my mom, best friend, aunt, doctors, and nurses. My child's father was not there, and because of the history between us during my pregnancy, I honestly didn't want him there. During the nine months of pregnancy, I worked full-time, went to college full-time, and even graduated with my Bachelor's five days before giving birth. Even with all these accomplishments, it still didn't stop the fact I was in the hospital room holding a brand new beautiful baby and the biological father was not there.

After phone conversations, DNA tests to prove this child was his, and many hurtful encounters after that---I will admit I became a very wounded, bitter, and enraged baby mama. The type of baby mama that when he would call to ask about his child, I would say, "That would be $50 because knowing information about your child costs." Yeah, I used to say things like that. Mean selfish things, but hey...it was how I was feeling! I was feeling alone, raising this child all by myself, stressed about finding a job straight out of school, and making sure I'm a great mother to this child now being raised by a single parent.

DELISA NEW WILLIAMS

    Let's just say being a single mother was not my freaking dream. Hell, I even told my child's father while I was pregnant that we should work it out and move in with each other, just so we can "try" to have a family. Talk about being desperate to have a family, but as a mother, you'll try to do whatever YOU think is right, just so YOU can create this fictional life for your child. I was willing to sike myself into "loving" this man, so I can have a pretend family, but Hallelujah he turned me down...thank God! Truly, I thank God that He doesn't answer ALL of our ridiculous prayers! However, my child's father knew I wasn't in love with him. He knew it was just a fling like the beginning of a Grease movie; you know where two love-birds John Travolta and Olivia John-Newton have the most adventurous and romantic summer of a lifetime. But my fairytale ended with me finding out I was pregnant by a man who spent the first three months of my pregnancy begging me to get an abortion. Even after I got over the whole ordeal of us not being together for the sake of our child, moved on to a better job and a new boyfriend at the time, he still tried to break me and ruin my whole life. Although I moved on, the testimony of how I overcame through the strength of God being made perfect in my life during that time is a story for another book.

    To deal with the issues that stemmed from my child's father and being a single mother, I went to counseling for almost two years. During that time, I read books, did some self-reflecting, and received the healing necessary to free me from the pain of my past hurt and open the doors to becoming a wife to an amazing man whom I've been with for almost eight years now, and looking forward to forever. I thought my journey of dealing with hurt and bitterness was over until the man I love and said "I do" to had two sons in his life from two different women, and then, the Deja Vu and rollercoaster of hurt, pain, brokenness, and anger resurfaced...but to another degree. In this situation, I was on the outside looking in, and I was able to clearly see my actions and self-reflect on the part I played in my very own situation.

    It's interesting how you can't see the wrong in a situation until you're standing on the outside looking in, and from that

NO LONGER AM I A BABY MAMA

point of view is where you begin to open the door to understanding and forgiveness, so you can be fully transformed, healed, and move forward in life. I dealt with child support concerning my husband and honestly, being a single mother who NEVER received any form of payment for supporting my child---I am a huge freaking fan of child support! I believe if you can't get consistent support (being financial or time), a mother should fight for the child's right. Because my situation with my daughter's father involved some criminal and legal issues, I opted to not have child support. Yeah, I know what you're thinking...she wrote a book about healing and forgiveness and her child's biological father did prison time! How could that be... you ask? Well, because just like Jesus had to forgive those who persecuted and crucified Him as they know not what they do. I too, had to forgive my child's father and walk in forgiveness for what He did to me and my daughter as well. And because of that, I believe that's why God blessed me with the loving husband I have today, and my daughter has never lacked love in any department when it comes to having an upstanding father in her life! So, with child support payments, child support court, restraining orders, us not seeing our sons because their mothers were mad at us for whatever ridiculous reason that made sense to them, phone hang-ups, cuss outs... you name it. I endured and watched my husband suffer internally every day fighting our kids' mothers in and out of court when honestly, he just wanted to be a father. No one is a perfect parent. Even Mary got told off by Jesus when she came looking for him while he was preaching at the synagogue. Parents learn and parents grow, but fighting and arguing with one another truly doesn't hurt anyone but the child. I wrote this book in hopes to be a voice for the mother who just doesn't know how to be healed, but truly desires it. This book has real-life applications for you to grow up, be healed, and become the best mother God has created YOU to be.

    I believe in daily affirmations. I believe in counseling. Most of all, I believe in the Word of God, so including the scripture chart which has all the scriptures used in the book---is very, very necessary! Also, I love music and believe music is therapeutic and tells a story of healing and truth, which is why Erykah's song "Bag Lady" tells a story of brokenness, but also sheds light on the outcome of your future if you allow baggage to weigh you down in life. Everything mentioned in this book...I did, I witnessed, and I'm free. You might cry, do a lot of self-evaluation, and pray like you've never done before. How do I know? Because it's exactly what I had to do!! Now, it's your turn! It's time for you to embark on this journey with me, rid yourself of that stank attitude, and come on girl', let's be free!

Special Note to My Readers

I felt it was important to explain the reasoning behind this book. Being a previous baby momma myself, I realized the issues and behavior I was displaying, regarding my own personal situation, weren't good for me or my daughter—nor was it going to help my current relationship with my husband. I went to Amazon's website to find any literature I could on how to get rid of this attitude and hurt I was operating out of, but much to my dismay, I couldn't find anything that stood out. I didn't want to read a 400+ page book about self-help and healing.

I researched online and found websites mentioning all these 7-steps and 10-steps to healing practices. I didn't have time for that either. I felt 3-steps was too short, but 7 and 10 were too long...my opinion. But really, I just wanted to get the meat and potatoes of this thing and move forward. That's when I stumbled across this online article about spiritual and emotional healing by Brian Knack. See, I knew healing was in reach! It was quick and only had 5 steps. I figured that if I could start on Monday, and do one step a day, by Friday I would be healed.

After doing it myself, writing my own experiences, and with God adding some extra lessons and wisdom of His own, I was and am completely HEALED and ALL the way TOGETHER!! Thank God! Don't get me wrong, things still popped up and issues surfaced, but I was able to identify them, pray about it, and work it out! That's the key—being able to WORK it OUT!! I thought to myself, how many women are battling these same issues, and what if I could write a book that women can be healed in a week's time by activating their faith?

---

*baby mama or baby momma- /'baba'/ /'mäme/ noun
1. The mother of your child(ren), whom you did not marry.
2. The mother of your child(ren) with whom you are not currently involved. In addition; the mother of a man's biological child; especially: one who is not married to or in a long-term, intimate relationship with the child's father
First Known Use 1986

*Cited Merriam-Webster Dictionary - "baby mama"

NO LONGER AM I A BABY MAMA

***baby mama:**
A woman who has a child out of wedlock with a man. She may or may not be in a relationship with the man, but most of the time, she's not. She may think she has some sort of postion or leverage in the man's life, just because she had a child with the man, but all she is, is a baby mama, nothing else. Some baby mamas use the child as a pawn or weapon to "get what they want" from the child's father, IE: money, food, sex, etc. If the man is in a realtionship with a woman who has no children, the baby mama may become jealous and cause baby mama drama. Not all baby mama's are like that. The majority of them just act like they can control the man just because they had a seed with them, and make it difficult for the man and threaten to take the child away or sue for more child support if the baby mama doesn't get her way.

A term used to define an unmarried young woman (but can be a woman of any age) who has had a child. As mentioned before, most of the time, the term is used when it was simply a sexual relationship, compared to a one night stand or girlfriend. Usually this has a negative connotation, a lot of baby mamas are seen as desperate, gold digging, emotionally starved, shady women who had a baby out of spite or to keep a man. Sometimes they may act like this because of missed child support payments, unfulfilled promises by the father, or because their still having convenient sex with one another. Either or both may exist in any situation.

*Cited www.urbandictionary.com - "baby mama"

"I am an ATMOSPHERE CHANGER. I am a HELPER. I am a CHANGE AGENT. What's important about life to me is I want to make a difference, I want to help your CROOKED WAYS *become* STRAIGHT, your BLURRED VISION *becoming* 20/20, and your PURPOSE *being fulfilled as well as mine.* I'm here to make an IMPACT *on the* WORLD *and most importantly make my Father proud of me!*"

– *DeLisa New Williams* M.B.A.
AUTHOR, INSPIRATIONAL SPEAKER, ENTREPRENEUR, AND MEDIA PERSONALITY

INTRODUCTION

I'm the one Pregnant, not you!!

Whether your results came from a missed period, over the counter pregnancy test, or doctor visit, the proof was there that YOU, the mother, were pregnant and didn't get this way on your own. You had help—perhaps a man...in some cases many men. Yes, on more than several occasions throughout the history of time, women were not fully knowledgeable of the father of their child. If you are shocked by this statement, please check your local listings for the Maury Povich show and watch an infamous episode of "YOU ARE NOT THE FATHER".

In any event, if the father is known or unknown, there's one thing for sure that we all know...the baby is yours. Yes, this child is yours. The child is yours to love, to bond with, to nurture, and for you to experience God's great gift. Do you know that you were chosen by God to bring forth life? This gift isn't given to every woman. According to the National Survey of Family Growth, there are 7.3 million women between the ages of 15-44 with impaired fecundity (impaired ability to have children)1. WOW!!! That's the number of women who want what you have—a child—but are incapable of bringing forth the gift. Aren't you beyond blessed?

 The weekly doctor visits, bladder pains, crazy food cravings, weight gain, self-esteem issues, and stress are just a few things women go through during their nine months of pregnancy. Also, these events are even more stressful if you're doing it all alone. By alone, I mean without the biological father being physically present, because you know God never left you. According to the Word of God, Hebrews 13:5 NIV: "...never will I leave you; never will I forsake you." He was there during your tears and smiles, pain and joy, good and bad times. The biological father may be gone, but the heavenly father still remains. The majority of my nine months was spent without the father of my child, and thankfully, I had a support team of family and friends that stepped in where he ran off.

 I actually thought I was kind of lucky, considering a close friend of mine experienced infidelity and verbal abuse during her first pregnancy from the father of her child, and he practically was with her every day. It kind of validated my reason for why I didn't care if he was a part of my child's life, or not. I believed I was all my child ever needed. I considered taking care of my child alone as being normal because that was my family background. I now know that I operated out of selfishness. I was wrong. Anytime, you do something for personal gain at the expense of others, it's wrong. God says in Philippians 2:3-4 ESV: "Do nothing from rivalry or conceit, but in humility count others more significant than yourselves. Let each of you look not only to his own interests, but also to the interests of others."

 As mothers, we cannot only look to our own interests, but to the interests of the father and the child. Your child deserves every right to be loved by his/her father and/or paternal family. Your child deserves the right to experience that bond and relationship. It is not the mother's right, nor anyone else's for that matter, to take that away unless physical, mental, verbal, and emotional abuse is involved—what would be defined as 'the serious stuff'. Therefore, the minor things, like the father cheated on you, OR he doesn't want a relationship anymore, OR he didn't give you any money when you asked, are not justifications for punishing your child's father away and not letting him spend time with his child.

Take this time to evaluate yourself as a person, a woman, a mother, and most importantly, a child of God. In all things, we should acknowledge Him and allow God to get the glory out of every good and bad situation. It is not up to the mother to be vindictive and deceitful. In this book, I pray God will minister to your spirit and open your eyes to His purpose for you, your child, and the father. You truly need to see God in this and allow God to bring forth a beautiful, cordial, and respectful relationship between you and the father.

For fathers, take this time to understand the mother of your child/ren. Use the knowledge in this book to guide you on how to go to God on her behalf. You have a responsibility to God, your children, and yourself to desire more for your child's mother. The bible says the strong shall bear the infirmities of the weak, and as a man, it is your duty to pray, and even fast if necessary, to help your child's mother receive healing. In all situations, before pointing the finger, evaluate yourself.

DELISA NEW WILLIAMS

*Can you identify with the introduction?
Write your thoughts/reflections/ or questions below....

"Your willingness to look at your DARKNESS is what EMPOWERS you to change."
- Iyanla Vanzant

INSPIRATIONAL SPEAKER, LAWYER, TEACHER, AUTHOR, LIFE COACH AND TV PERSONALITY

#NoLongerAmIABabyMama

CHAPTER 1

ADMITTANCE: I don't have the problem: He does!!

According to my intensive research on the steps to spiritual healing, the main thing I found in common was admittance. For example, reading an excerpt from Joyce Meyers *Three Steps to Emotional Healing That Lasts,* she says, "Nobody can be set free from a problem until they're willing to admit they have one." There's a process to being healed and ridding yourself of certain negative behaviors and mentalities. In this section, we're going to cover the first step, which is admittance.

ADMITTANCE
You must first admit that there is an issue to get to the root of change. Spiritual and emotional wounds are sometimes so heavy and painful feelings that you need to look deeper within and ask God to show you the root to bring forth the change necessary to grow. You have to admit, there are some reasons why you're acting the way you are toward the biological father of your children. Whether you are denying the father his rights, keeping him from seeing his child, or perpetuating senseless arguments, it is due to hurt that lies inside of you. Have you ever heard the saying, "Hurt people hurt people?" Think about

it. Usually, when you are hurting inside, it's only natural to want others around you to hurt as badly as you do, especially the person that may be responsible for the pain you're experiencing.

I can attest to this from my own personal experience. The biological father of my child confessed his love for me on a daily basis. He wrote love letters to me, and talked to me on the phone until we reached that giddish, childlike stage where we were holding the phone saying, "You hang up! No, you hang up! On three hang up!" But, when I revealed that I was pregnant, he had an epitome. He realized that he no longer wanted to be with me. Here I was five months pregnant with my first child, and the man I *knew*, who gave me an overwhelming amount of attention on a daily basis, *disappeared*. I was lost and confused! I made it my business to intentionally get back at him by ignoring phone calls, graduating from college, and giving birth to my daughter without informing him, all the while believing I wasn't hurting on the inside. You too may even have convinced yourself that you are not hurting. If you've said things like, "It really doesn't matter that much," "I'm okay with us not being together," or "I'm all my child ever needs." You're lying to yourself, you're living a façade, and you're in denial.

You must first admit that you're hurting. The relationships today involving "baby momma" and "baby daddy" drama aren't healthy for the parents or the child/ren. It is not okay for you, as the mother, to have pain inside when you are thinking of the biological father of your child. It is not okay for you to be jealous, bitter, or even envious of him for leaving you, moving on, or running away from his responsibility (if this is the case). It's not okay for you to bribe the biological father into being with you or buying things for you in order to be with his child/ren. You have to admit that this is not right! Your ill feelings, your intense pain, your substantial confusion, and your deep hurt…Every part of you deserves healing and deserves to be free from the strong holds.

The Gospel of St. John 20:23(Jubilee Bible 2000) says that we have to release the sins of others if we are going to be released. This means that if we do not forgive others, then the very thing we have become victimized by will become part of our lives. *You will not, I repeat will not, gain anything in life by hurting others.* You may have gotten temporary gratification when you hung up the phone, cussed him out, or kept the baby away from him while he begged and pleaded for his child, or you may have even took him to child support unnecessarily. Whatever you have done with ill intentions may look like you've won the battle, but in reality, you have lost the war.

Pray this prayer on Admittance:

Lord, help me at this time in my life. Help me to see the part I've played in this. Open my eyes, Oh Lord, so I can be held accountable for my own actions. I am no longer in bondage to this "baby momma" spirit. The spirit of vindictiveness, envy, bitterness, and hurt no longer reside in me. Lord, I am tired of being hurt. Take this hurt away God. Show me how to live my life better as a mother to my child/ren and most of all as a woman of God. Show me how I look to you, so I can see what you see and become who you want me to be. Amen.

NO LONGER AM I A BABY MAMA

Can you identify with Chapter 1: Admittance?
Write your thoughts/reflections/ or questions below....

_____
_____
_____
_____
_____
_____
_____
_____
_____
_____
_____
_____
_____
_____
_____
_____
_____
_____
_____
_____
_____
_____
_____

After reading this book, you may want to seek wise counseling to further understand where the pain stems from and take a stand in facing your spiritual and emotional hurt.

Ain't NOTHING *coming easily in this life. Sometimes you gotta* WORK, *you gotta* GROW *and it gotta* HURT...
—Jill Scott
AWARD WINNING SINGER-SONGWRITER AND ACTRESS

#NoLongerAmIABabyMama

Chapter 2
God, SHOW me where this is coming from?

DISCOVERY
This step is about discovering the cause of the spiritual and emotional pain involved in this baby momma lifestyle. In 1 Timothy 6:10a KJV, the Bible states that the love of money is the root of all evil. Money isn't the root of all evil, but the love of it is. Why would one love money? Think about it. Let's discover this issue together. One could love money because they grew up in poverty and went hungry many nights wishing they had food; therefore, their love of money came about from survival. Or, growing up, one looked at people with money as powerful and successful; therefore, their love of money correlated with power and control. They would hurt family and friends just to get a taste of success. So, the love of money stems from a spiritual and emotional wound from their past. In this chapter, we're going to look at ourselves and ask God to help us discover the root of bitterness, anger, jealousy, vindictiveness, hurt, and the hatred that lies inside.

The significance of identifying where this hurt comes from is crucial to the healing process. We **have** to get to the root of the problem! If we do not find the cause, the same attitudes and behaviors will be perpetuated in similar circumstances. As time goes by, you'll just keeping adding more baggage and more of your issues with each new problem that arises between yourself and the biological father. For example, you and the biological father begin arguing over what school the child should attend. "Why are your child's clothes dirty?" "Why is your son's hair not cut?" All the way to the famous line, "Why are you bringing my daughter around your girlfriends?" The reality of the matter is, there is an underlying issue present that keeps getting covered by all these other insignificant problems. Listen to me as I say this to you, YOU HAVE TO GET TO THE ROOT BEFORE YOU CAN MOVE ON AND BECOME HEALED!

<u>Neo-soul singer, Erykah Badu[2] said it best in her song "Bag Lady."</u> Here's an excerpt from the song, but please take time to familiarize yourself with the lyrics because the words really resonate with the information in this chapter.

One day all them bags gon' get in your way, so pack light,
Bag lady you gon' miss your bus
You can't hurry up, 'cause you got too much stuff
When they see you coming, (men) take off running
From you it's true, oh yes they do

Carrying baggage, hurt, and issues cannot only physically hurt you, but it can hurt you spiritually and emotionally. Not letting go of this pain doesn't hurt anybody but you in the end—not the biological father, not the child, just you! James 4:1-3 NIV: "[1]What causes fights and quarrels among YOU? Don't they come from YOUR desires that battle within YOU? [2]YOU desire but do not have, so YOU kill. YOU covet but YOU cannot get what YOU want, so YOU quarrel and fight. YOU do not have because YOU do not ask God. [3]When YOU ask, YOU do not receive, because YOU ask with wrong motives, that YOU may spend what YOU get on your pleasures." If you keep on operating out of this baby momma spirit of being mean, hurtful, angry, vengeful, and spiteful, all those issues are going to get in your way and prevent you from your destiny, from your God-given purpose. Let it go. Let it all go and give it to God. Don't carry this heavy load full of mess, take the lesson you were supposed to learn from it, drop the other bad stuff, and give it to God.

Matthew 11:28-30 NIV: "Come to me, all you who are weary and burdened, and I will give you rest.²⁹ Take my yoke upon you and learn from me, for I am gentle and humble in heart, and you will find rest for your souls.³⁰ For my yoke is easy and my burden is LIGHT." With all the issues you are carrying around, you will miss the promise that God has on your life. You will begin to rot from the inside out. Your relationships with people, including your child, will suffer. People will run from you and not want to talk to you because you will try to put all your issues and hurt on them. It'll consume you and become all you'll think and talk about. You will ruin relationships and possibly lose some of them, because no one wants to be around people with issues unless they too have the same issues themselves. Proverbs 22:24 ESV: "Make no friendship with a man given to anger, nor go with a wrathful man."

All those negative spirits and things you carry around do more harm than good. In the physical sense, you only see one of you, but there are many spirits attached to you because of all the issues you won't let go of. When you hold onto these spirits, they will overcrowd your life because they follow you wherever you go. When you eat dinner, those spirits are right there at the table. I can remember my family having dinner at Red Lobster. I was on my way to join them, when I received a phone call from my mother stating that my child's biological father was in restaurant with *his new baby, other baby mama, and older child* celebrating the *new* addition to their *family*. I wanted so badly to drive to that Red Lobster and flip tables. I envisioned myself picking up the steak knife from the table and stabbing him multiple times. My breathing became labored, and I began to cry hysterically! Don't get me wrong here, the situation surrounding my child and her biological father is an *extreme* circumstance, but the healing process and spiritual warfare is still applicable.

Even when you go to bed at night, and you are in a comfortable slumber, those spirits attached to you are tucked in nice and tight under those covers with you! But with God, He will remove all that pain and release you from those negative spirits so you can be set free. John 8:36 NIV: "So if the Son sets you free, you will be free indeed."

Personal Testimony Time – Do not let the devil shut down your testimony!

<u>Pray this prayer on Discovery:</u>
Lord, I thank you for allowing me to discover my issues and for showing me the part I have played in this situation. Show me, Father, how to love people even if I don't like what they say or do. Show me how to get to the root of what's really bothering me and let it go. Lord rid me of my issues. I no longer want them! Teach me how to walk in love and teach me how to be free from my past hurt, childhood experiences, and bad memories. Lord help me! I thank you in advance for being here with me and having me discover my truth. Amen.

NO LONGER AM I A BABY MAMA

*Can you identify with Chapter 2: Discovery?
Write your thoughts/reflections/ or questions below....

_____
_____
_____
_____
_____
_____
_____
_____
_____
_____
_____
_____
_____
_____
_____
_____
_____
_____
_____
_____
_____
_____
_____

I wanted to HURT *you the way you hurt me, but I couldn't* CUT *you & tend to my own* WOUNDS.

You can get EVEN *or you can get* BETTER. *You can't do* BOTH *at the same time.*

—Sarah Jakes Roberts
BUSINESS WOMAN, WRITER, AND SPEAKER

#NoLongerAmIABabyMama

Chapter 3

Cleanse me from the inside out

Cleansing

My husband is a paramedic, and he brings his work home with him from time to time. Whenever one of our four children hurts themselves, he decides to use medical terminology that no one understands, and it just cracks me up. He ends up complicating the simplest things with these jazzy medical words, when all the children really want to do is run and put a Band-Aid on to cover the pain. This is especially true for my oldest daughter, who is such a big cry baby! My husband always goes for the peroxide even though it may burn her a bit. He puts peroxide on her wounds and reassures her that it's necessary to clean the wound first before we just "run and put a Band-Aid on it". Great lesson, right? How many times have we just put Band-Aids on situations thinking it will heal on its own or it'll cover up the scar. Only to find out later we've just masked the problem, and probably made it worse. I mean think about it, you could have an infection, and the wound could spread. You could even possibly be hospitalized; all because your wound wasn't properly cleansed from the beginning!

This is the same way we treat OUR hurt, OUR pain, OUR disgust, and OUR issues. We'll mask our hurt and pain by saying "I'm okay," "I don't want him anymore," "I just want him to be here for my child," or "I don't care about him at all." You cannot keep living a façade. These things you are telling yourself are all lies from the pit of hell. YOU are not okay and YOU do care—well, at least you should. In 1 John 4:20 NIV Version, it reads: "Whoever claims to love God yet hates a brother or sister is a liar. For whoever does not love their brother and sister, whom they have seen, cannot love God, whom they have not seen." So seriously, how can you love God, whom you've never seen, but hate your brother whom you have seen? This is a "get yourself together" book with biblical principles, but I could easily tell you how to do it the world's way. You've probably already done it! Or you may be doing it right now as you read this book. I could tell you to go to court, get your money, stop talking to your child's father forever, and wish revenge on his life for as long as he lives, but what good does that do you? While he's being tormented here on earth, your torment will come later from the unforgiveness and uncleanliness in your heart. You'll have to answer to God! I know you may be hurt, but you have to act in love. You must forgive in spite of everything that has happened between the two of you.

Cleansing from the inside may require a fast.[4] A fast is not a diet; it involves abstaining from food while focusing on prayer. This can mean refraining from snacks between meals, skipping one or two meals a day, abstaining only from certain foods, or a total fast from all food for an entire day or longer. If, the majority of the time, negative thoughts come to your mind about your child's father, or you constantly speak negatively to him, or you all argue a lot, you may need to seek God and see if He requires a fast from you to discipline you in necessary areas. You need to hear directly from God and let Him show you how to talk to your child's father, and give you direction concerning the issue, because every situation is different.

Ultimately, forgiveness is the key to everything. While doing my research on spiritual cleansing, I stumbled across this scripture, and it just blew me out the water and opened my eyes! Take a look at Ephesians 4:26, 27 in the TLB Version, it reads: "If you are angry, don't sin by nursing your grudge. Don't let the sun go down with you still angry—get over it quickly;[27] for when you are angry, you give a mighty foothold to the devil." WHAT?!! You just read it right here from the Lord's book, "Be angry, but don't go nursing your hurt and your grudges against your child's father. Get over it because the longer you hold on to it, the longer it will have a hold on you!" YOU CANNOT AFFORD TO GIVE THE DEVIL ANY SPOT, CORNER, ROOM, OR SHELF IN YOUR LIFE! Stop it! As you continue to read Ephesians 4:31-32 TLB, it also says: "Stop being mean, bad-tempered, and angry. Quarreling, harsh words, and dislike of others should have no place in your lives."

Once Jesus cleanses you from the inside out, you'll see the change in how you treat your child's father, or even how you treat your children. You'll begin to see the change in how you treat other fathers or just men period. You will see an inward change as well as an outward change. You'll smile more, laugh more, pray more, and best of all love more. Your children deserve __all__ of you cleansed—not some of you clean, some of you bruised, and the rest battered. God is the ultimate cleanser.

Pray this prayer on Cleansing:
Lord cleanse me. I want to be cleansed by you, Father. I want to only have pure intentions and pure thoughts when it comes to my child's father. Lord show me how I should talk to him and show me how to pray for him. Forgive me Lord for all the negative words I've said, wrong things I've done, my spitefulness, and me just being plain ole mean. It wasn't right of me to behave that way. Lord, forgive my child's father for the things he's done to hurt me whether intentionally or unintentionally. Forgive him Lord and Bless him. Show both of us how to be great parents to our children. Show both of us how to be pleasant and kind to one another. In Jesus Name. Amen.

DELISA NEW WILLIAMS

***Can you identify with Chapter 3: Cleansing?
Write your thoughts/reflections/ or questions below....**

It all starts with YOU. YOU'RE *the temple and you have control.* YOU'RE *in a bad situation? It's up to* YOU *to get out of it.* YOU *can't give another human the responsibility of* YOUR *happiness.*
-*Taraji P. Henson*
AWARD WINNING ACTRESS, SINGER, AND AUTHOR

#NoLongerAmIABabyMama

Chapter 4

If you want to RECEIVE, You have to BELIEVE

Believe/Receive

Do you really want to be set free? Do you want to be healed? Or do you like playing the victim? These are very critical questions regarding YOUR healing. Do you enjoy telling people your sad story? Embellishing it a bit! Do you find joy in telling your side of the story so you can get sympathy, or be a part of the SINGLE MOM-I HATE MY BABY DADDY/EX CLUB featuring you, the Club President? You do it all, right? When the baby's sick who's going to the hospital? You! Who pays for daycare or after school? You! Who does the grocery shopping? You! Who provides transportation to school? Washes clothes? Who pays for dance lessons? Who foots the bill for basketball lessons? Who helps with homework? Who's in attendance for teacher conferences? YOU, YOU, YOU! Yes, we get it! You are a wonderful, amazing, and strong woman. You are doing everything in your power for your child, yes *your* child! NOT for the father's doing or his praise, but for your child. Everything that you're doing is for your child's well-being, for their future.

Being a victim comes in handy when we don't feel like changing or growing. Why would you want to move ahead in life? You enjoy being here, pointing the finger, playing the blame game, and going tit-for-tat. It gives you the energy and ammunition you need to survive. You've validated your way of thinking by what you do for your children, and simply, this is NOT right. What's amazing about playing the victim is oftentimes (more than you think), you're really the villain. You choose not to forgive or "let it go" because playing the victim is like fuel to a fire. Victims use words like "should," "fair," and "right/wrong." Have you ever said to your child's father, "You should take her to the doctor when she's sick," or "It's not fair that I have to do everything for our child."

Here's another way to see if you're operating out of a victimized spirit—check your surroundings! Do you hang around bitter single moms, or do you have a circle of single moms who struggle with the same issues you do with your child's father? Do you tend to get advice from other women who seek revenge on their child's father? It boils down to asking yourself, do I want to be a victim or a victor? In Romans 8:37 (Good News Translation): "No, in all these things we have complete victory through Him who loved us!" This scripture says that if we believe in Jesus Christ, we are victorious in EVERYTHING!! You have a choice in the matter! No one can take your choice from you; God gives it to you freely. You have to determine whether you will be the one to give it away. Am I going to choose to be a victor, or am I choosing to be the VICTIM? Because what you fail to realize is that whatever the child's father IS NOT doing or HAS NOT DONE, he still has to answer to God for that…not you! In Galatians 6:7(NIV): "Do not be deceived: God cannot be deceived. A man reaps what he sows."

Another reason why you may not want to receive healing and be set free is because that means you would have to internalize some things about yourself. You may even have to identify issues with your parents or family members, and that would create a deeper hurt. In order to receive TRUE healing with your child's father, you need to get to the core and understanding where your hurt comes from. This will help in the healing process, because the one thing you don't want is a false sense of being healed—only to realize in months or even years down the road that you ended up right where you started...broken and hurt. You'll just repeat the next chapter in your life with another guy, or you'll sow all those seeds of hurt and pain into your child. What needs to be understood more than anything is, NO MORE HURT and NO MORE PAIN.

    Believe me, I know that everyone reading this book has their own story. Your child's father might have left you and the kids for another woman, and you had no clue. You might have even been abused by your child's father, and had no choice but to get out of a deadly situation. You could have had a one night stand, or a homie-lover-friend...the list could go on and on. I promise you, I get it! I want you to know that this book is solely about YOU! YOUR healing, YOUR deliverance, and YOUR freedom. You deserve all that God has for you, down to the last drop. You have to believe that you are better than whatever this issue is that has affected you. You are worth so much more than walking around in the pain and hurt of your past.

    Your child's father may not be the BEST father in your eyes, but that isn't your issue. You have the power to believe he will be better! Believing the best for your child's father and releasing him unto Christ is just as believing the best for your child. You want your child's father to prosper, because when he prospers, your child will prosper. When you believe and have faith that the child's biological father will be kind and better himself, you're actually praying for your child's future as well. You do not want your children to have to deal with anything negative that might be lingering behind from their father.

    You have to believe for the best, because this is when your breakthrough will come. Your release, your healing, your being set-free comes from believing and having faith that your situation will change. Just tell yourself, "It's getting better already!" When you speak daily affirmations, you will begin to see things shift in your situation with your child's biological father, but most importantly within yourself. Things won't upset you like they used to, and you won't even have the urge to argue anymore. More laughter and less arguing! When a situation occurs between you and the father—him being late, broken promises, he doesn't have any money, or whatever the issue is—it won't even faze you AT ALL.

    The bible says in Proverbs 18:21: "Death and life are in the power of the tongue, and those who love it will eat its fruits." Do you understand what this scripture is saying? If you speak negativity, death, things that are NOT good at all, honey, you eat those words, every bit of them. When you say your child's father is trifling, unworthy, a sack of crap, butthole, oh I can go on...those are words coming out of your mouth and you EAT them. Now what's produced from your fruit when you speak those words? Bad relationships, hatred, arguments, revenge, and remember the scripture we read earlier...whatever you sow, you reap! Therefore, everything you've ever said and done, which you know in your heart was not right, YOU will reap. For the sake of your future, and your children's future and their well-being, it's vital to be aware of your words and actions.

    Since we've talked about sowing and reaping bad seeds, how do you sow and reap good seeds? Seriously sowing seeds of good deeds or kind and pleasant conversation is an essential key to your freedom and healing. I'm not making this up, trust and believe God has many ways to help you get to this place of healing. In Genesis 26:12 ESV, "And Isaac sowed in that land and reaped in the same year a hundredfold. The Lord blessed him..." Now I don't know about you, but I don't have time to play with MY healing, ME being set free, and ME reaping from God; so if your Heavenly Father tells you that if you sow into something you'll reap it in the same year...well honey you better get to sowing! If you and your child's father aren't on good speaking terms, have a positive adult meeting/conversation in front of the kids to show the growth between you both. Invite him (and his wife and/or other kids) to a family gathering or get together to show how you two can be in the same room and it not be any strife or tension between you two. If you don't believe your child's father is a good father, buy him a Father's Day card that has positive words inside of the man/father your kids would like and need him to become. If it's his birthday, take your child to get him a birthday card or even a present. Going with your child to pick out a card shows you that you're getting close to your healing, but it also shows your child/ren that Mommy and Daddy can work it out and finally get along. It shows the child that they should honor their parents regardless of the circumstance because if they don't see you honoring their father eventually they won't either and it could be disastrous for you as well because next thing you know, you'll be the one being dishonored.

Now don't get caught all caught up in thinking, "well he doesn't buy me a card so why do I need to buy him one?". That type of thinking surely will have you dealing with years of bitterness. Here you are up here trying to get free and you're worrying about a $1.99 card...girl, bye! This is your moment to shine! Your moment to free and your moment to stand on God's Word and show that you don't have any bitterness uprooted you. That you are totally free! Hebrews 12:15 (NIV) See to it that no one falls short of the grace of God and that no bitter root grows up to cause trouble and defile many. You want all that bitterness, hurt, and pain gone FOREVER so wasting time on what your child father does or doesn't do, truly shouldn't have any connection whatsoever once God has spoken. Point blank and Period!

Pray this prayer on believing and receiving:
Lord please change my negative speaking and thinking to words and thoughts that are pleasing to you, Father. Lord, I pray my child isn't affected by what they've seen or heard and that I can be a great example to them. I believe in you Lord, all things are new. Renew my mind Father. I want to only think pos-

itive thoughts and speak positively about my relationship with my child's father. Lord I am open to correction from you God, and I need you desperately to show me how to speak loving and kind words regardless of what my situation may look like, I will hope in you and believe in you that things will turn around for the better. In Jesus name, Amen.

Can you identify with Chapter 4: Believing/Receiving?
Write your thoughts/reflections/ or questions below....

STRENGTH *is measured by how many times you* FALL, *and* TRUST GOD *enough to get back up* AGAIN!

—*Nina Michelle Blakey* M.A.T & M.Ed
AUTHOR OF "KEEPING IT 100" & "ADDICTED TO LOVE"

CHAPTER 5
You have to be STRONG

Ephesians 6:10-12 King James Version (KJV): "[10]Finally, my brethren, be strong in the Lord, and in the power of his might. [11] Put on the whole armour of God that ye may be able to stand against the wiles of the devil. [12] For we wrestle not against flesh and blood, but against principalities, against powers, against the rulers of the darkness of this world, against spiritual wickedness in high places."

So, you've finally made it here. You didn't drop the book or throw it away. Smile and take a deep breath because this shows your determination for CHANGE...Your desire to be BETTER! Wanting this, takes a lot of strength. You will need plenty of strength to combat the thoughts that will occur after finishing this book, or situations that will arise between you and your child's father. You have to know that the devil doesn't want you and your child's father to be peaceful. Peace belongs to God. The Bible says in Proverbs 16:7: "When a man's ways please the Lord, He makes even his enemies to be at peace with him." Is God really saying that He will make your enemies be at peace with you when you please Him? That seems so easy, right?

Listen, you might not consider your child's father an enemy; however, the two of you aren't seeing eye to eye in situations that present themselves. You need to make sure you are pleasing to God in your actions, your thoughts, and most importantly your words, and watch how God will turn that situation around for you. Yes! Just for you! Not your child's father or your children, but you! You need to know that it's all about you. This very book was written for you. You have to stay focused on the fact that you've invested in yourself. This is about you and your healing. Don't allow anything to tear down what you've built up.

You need to be strong when situations between you and your child's father don't go as expected or the way you planned. Don't lash out, seek revenge, or even harden your heart. You need to take deep breaths, look within yourself, and pray for strength to overcome, for victory. Without the strength of God, you will return to that dark and painful place of bitterness, jealousy, hatred, and anything else the devil wants to attach to you. You say to yourself that you do more work than your child's father, you're the one that's there all the time with the kids, you're the full-time parent, and he's just part-time. Even with that being said, it's not by your might that you're an awesome parent. It's not your riches, wealth, education, etc. You are who you are because of the strength of God. How dare you cast judgement on anybody because of their failures or shortcomings? You have the job you have because God is helping you take care of your children. You have the house you're in because of God, and if you're living up to your expectations with your career or lifestyle in general, you have some self-reflection to do—that doesn't have anything to do with your child's father.

You need supernatural strength to stay in this place of peace and serenity because trust me, the enemy will try all he can in his power to throw you off, but you can't let him win. What if it was God's plan for the seed to just be created, and for your child's father to have nothing to do with the child at all,

OR what if God is using you to show your child's father how to actually be a father—especially if he never had a father of his own. However, in order to show someone anything, you'll need to be patient and kind. God won't change any situation for the better unless you humble yourself and become more patient and kind...point blank period!!

    I mean, there are so many reasons of what could be, what is, and what should be, but the fact of the matter is, whatever your situation is right now with your child's father, you will need to be strong to handle it. The issues that stem between you and your child's father is not normal. Fighting, arguing, cursing each other out, calling each other names...do you think that's a normal relationship? It isn't! Even if you just hate your child's father, dislike him in anyway, THAT IS NOT NORMAL!! You need strength to pray against those feelings you have towards him and ask God to take away those violent thoughts/behaviors he has towards you, or you have towards him. Earlier, I gave you a scripture, in Ephesians 6:12; but, I'm going to give it to you again from the Message Version, and I pray it truly speaks to your spirit and breaks this fight you have between you and child's father, or better yet the fight you're having internally within yourself, down completely. (My commentary is in RED)

    And that about wraps it up. **God is strong, and He wants you strong.** (PERIOD! God doesn't want you suffering and hurting in this relationship between you and your child's father) **So take everything the Master has set out for you, well-made weapons of the best materials.** (What are the best materials you ask? The Bible, books on healing, spiritual counseling, heck even this book you are reading now; these are all materials that God has given you to fight this stank baby momma mentality!) **And put them to use so you will be able to stand up to everything the Devil throws your way.** (Oh, so you really thought this was just all your baby daddy's doing? He's the one that hates you, he's the one that doesn't want a relationship with the child, he's the one that's always broke or doesn't recognize your

NO LONGER AM I A BABY MAMA

value as a mother...NEWSFLASH, there is a devil. A devil that loves to see you angry and hurting, and he'll do anything possible to continue to make that happen. He loves to see you mad about the silliest things: money, pickup/drop off times, keeping the child, etc. And keep this in mind, every time, you all angry or you get pissed off at him, you're not pleasing God, you're making the devil extra happy and you might as well throw him a party because he just set you up!!) **This is no afternoon athletic contest that we'll walk away from and forget about in a couple of hours. This is for keeps, a life-or-death fight to the finish against the Devil and all his angels.** (Your reward won't come overnight, but if you fight tonight, that will be a start. You need peace in your life forever, not just one day. You deserve happiness and that's going to take some praying, believing, apologizing, forgiving, and even fasting. You want a better relationship between you and child's father that's solely about the child, go on a fast and watch God MOVE!! Because remember you are not fighting your child's father, you are fighting the devil and his angels who could care less about you and your child.)

Moments of Realness

What do you want? Is it validation, a reward of some kind, or would you like a day named after you? What is it that you want? Yes, you have the right to be angry because the situation between you and your child's father is messed up. It's damaged, unbreakable, unforgivable even...to you. Even with everything that has happened to you and your child/ren, even with all the lies, mistakes, and excuses that were told, it DOES NOT warrant you the right to own this hurt and anger inside and act on it.

This book would not be complete without my very own personal testimony. I once was a baby momma. I once did everything that I'm writing about; therefore, I am speaking from experience. If for some reason I did not experience first-hand, I experienced second-hand. In order for God to do His perfect work in me, I had to be healed. I had to be healed in Jesus name and free from all the past issues and hurt I endured. I went to a therapist consistently for over a year to begin my healing process. Through counselling, I was able to see and work through the underlying issues that were masked by everyday life. It's easy to keep your child from their father when you don't want to be bothered, but unless your child is in a dangerous, threatening, abusive situation, that is not right! You have to work it out! Not just for your child's sake, but for you! When you're able to look back at it one day and laugh because you know you've conquered the battle and won the war. I would not be the wife I am today if I did not let go of the hurt and pain I experienced while being a baby momma and accept the love from my husband, truly trusting him wholeheartedly without dumping my issues on him from the situation with my child's biological father.

#NLAIABM

31 Days of Positive Affirmations for Moms

1 • God's love is working through me now and always.

2 • All my thoughts, words, and actions are divinely guided.

3 • I forgive quickly and easily because I know forgiveness is the key to my happiness.

4 • I let go of fear. I let go of pain. I let go of hurt, and I choose to live in love.

5 • I ask for forgiveness from all those whom I may have wronged and forgive all those who may have wronged me. All is well.

6 • I am made whole and complete.

7 • God is my source.

8 • A river of compassion washes away my anger and replaces it with love.

9 • Happiness is a choice, and I choose to be happy.

10 • My kids looking up to me recognizes my worth. My children admire me.

11 • I feel joy and contentment in this moment right now knowing my child's father and I are getting along better daily.

12 • Don't be bitter...be better!

13 • The very thing that hurts me today, will make me so much stronger tomorrow.

14 • I am a better woman and mother than I was yesterday.

15 • My child is a blessing and any relationship that stems from them is a blessing also.

16 • Jesus is the vine and I am the branch...I can do NOthing without Him.

17 • My perspective changes TODAY!!

18 • I appreciate where I am right now, and I will continue to strive for greatness.

19 • I am right where God wants me to be. He is in control!

20 • I am made in God's image.

21 • I will give it my ALL instead of giving IN.

22 • I will not take things personally.

23 • Today is a NEW day. A day for me to right all my wrongs.

24 • I forgive myself and set myself FREE!

25 • I deserve the best, and I accept only what's best for me.

26 • It's okay to compromise because in the end, we both WIN!

27 • I listen to my kids with both my ears and my heart.

28 • If everyone else is suffering, while I'm winning...that's not really a victory!

29 • Get some rest today. It takes energy to be great!

30 • My life does not have to be PERFECT for it to be WONDERFUL. I determine that!

31 • Close my eyes and take a deep breath. Enjoy each moment today, because I am blessed and HIGHLY favored.

References

[1] www.cdc.gov, Source: Fertility, Family Planning, and Reproductive Health of U.S. Women: Data from the 2002 National Survey of Family Growth, tables 67, 69, 97.

[2] Badu, Erykah. "Bag Lady." By Erykah Badu and Andre Young. Mama's Gun. Motown Records, 2000. CD.

[3] www.healthland.time.com, 6 Breathing Exercises to Relax in 10 minutes or Less. Written by: Jordan Shakeshaft. October 08, 2012.

[4] http://christianity.about.com/od/whatdoesthebiblesay/a/spiritualfasting.htm, Spiritual
Fasting, What does the Bible Say About Spiritual Fasting? Written by: Mary Fairchild. 2014.

[5] http://www.urbandictionary.com/define.php?term=baby%20mama

[6] Knack, Brian. 5 Steps to Emotional and Spiritual Healing. 29 October 2009.

NO LONGER AM I BABY MOMMA
Scripture Chart

Intro	Chapter 1	Chapter 2	Chapter 3	Chapter 4	Chapter 5
Hebrews 13:5 NIV	St. John 20:23 Jubilee Bible 2000	II Timothy 6:10a KJV	I John 4:20 NIV	Romans 8:37 GNT	Ephesians 6:10-12 KJV
Phillipians 2:3-4 ESV		James 4:1-2 NIV	Ephesians 4:26, 27 TLB	Galatians 6:7 NIV	Proverbs 16:7 NKJV
		Matthew 11:28-30	Ephesians 4:31-32 TLB	Psalms 18:21 KJV	
		Proverbs 22:24 ESV		Genesis 26:12 ESV	
		John 8:36 NIV		Hebrews 12:15 NIV	

This is not a book for the woman who is trying to get back with her child's father. You won't read any tips on how to get him back; he's gone, he's free, and now it's your turn to be FREE as well.

With Love,
DeLisa New Williams

Meet DeLisa New Williams

"I came to set the people free. I can set you free if you wanna be free."

For further information, please contact **DeLisa New Williams by visiting**:

Website: www.delisanewwilliams.com
Facebook: www.facebook.com/delisanewwilliams
Instagram: www.instagram.com/delisanewwilliams
Twitter: www.twitter.com/delisadanielle_
YouTube: http://bit.ly/YouTube-delisanewwilliams

DELISA NEW WILLIAMS

Disclaimer: The information and solutions offered in this book are intended to serve as guidelines and suggestions for self-improvement. Please discuss specific issues, psychological, and spiritual information with your therapist.

Proverbs 19:20 ESV
Listen to advice and accept instruction, that you may gain wisdom in the future.

www.ingramcontent.com/pod-product-compliance
Lightning Source LLC
Chambersburg PA
CBHW071544080526
44588CB00011B/1787